21st Century Junior Library

DISCOVER THE STEGOSAURUS

Our Prehistoric World: Dinosaurs

Lucia Raatma

Published in the United States of America by:

CHERRY LAKE PRESS
2395 South Huron Parkway, Suite 200, Ann Arbor, Michigan 48104
www.cherrylakepress.com

Content Adviser: Gregory M. Erickson, PhD, Dinosaur Paleontologist, Department of Biological
Science, Florida State University, Tallahassee, Florida

Reading Adviser: Marla Conn, ReadAbility, Inc.

Cherry Lake Press is an imprint of Cherry Lake Publishing Group.

Library of Congress Cataloging-in-Publication Data has been filed and is available at catalog.loc.gov.

Cherry Lake Press would like to acknowledge the work of the Partnership for 21st Century Learning, a Network
of Battelle for Kids. Please visit http://www.battelleforkids.org/networks/p21 for more information.

Printed in the United States of America
Corporate Graphics

Note from publisher: Websites change regularly, and their future contents are outside of our control.
Supervise children when conducting any recommended online searches for extended learning opportunities.

CONTENTS

WHAT WAS A STEGOSAURUS?

Picture a dinosaur with huge plates on its back. That would be the *Stegosaurus*. It looked like no other dinosaur. The *Stegosaurus* lived about 150 million years ago. But like all other dinosaurs, the *Stegosaurus* is now extinct.

Many scientists believe *Stegosauruses* lived in groups.

Where did the name *Stegosaurus* come from? It is a Greek word that means "roofed lizard." Scientists named the dinosaur for the triangular plates along its back.

A *Stegosaurus* can be recognized by the plates on its back.

Think!

What other animals are covered with hard scales or plates? What are these body parts used for?

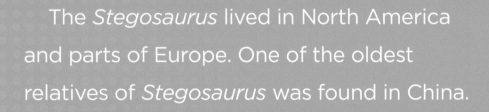

The *Stegosaurus* lived in North America and parts of Europe. One of the oldest relatives of *Stegosaurus* was found in China.

WHAT DID A STEGOSAURUS LOOK LIKE?

The *Stegosaurus* is best known for its plates. The large, flat, triangle-shaped plates were arranged in two rows. The dinosaur also had bony **scutes**. These were located on the sides of its neck and around its hips. They were similar to the bumps on an alligator's back.

Scientists have argued about how plates were positioned on a *Stegosaurus*'s back.

The *Stegosaurus* had an amazing tail! It was long and flexible, with four spikes on the end. Each spike was as long as 4 feet (1.2 meters). They may have helped the dinosaur protect itself from predators.

A *Stegosaurus* was almost as long as a school bus.

Look!

The next time you are in a parking lot, look at all the cars. Imagine if they were all dinosaurs! Which ones look like a *Stegosaurus*?

A *Stegosaurus* could be 26 to 30 feet (8 to 9 m) long. It was about 9 feet (2.7 m) tall. It weighed nearly 6,000 pounds (2,722 kilograms). That's as heavy as a large SUV or pickup truck!

This dinosaur also had strong, thick legs. Its front feet had five short toes. These toes looked like **hooves**. Its back feet had three toes. Though its body was huge, the *Stegosaurus*'s head was small. Its brain was only as big as a tennis ball!

The *Stegosaurus*'s brain was tiny for an animal of its size.

Create!

Draw a picture of a tennis ball. Think about how small it is. Now draw pictures of other items about the same size. Consider a baseball or a few walnuts. Can you believe that the *Stegosaurus* had a brain that small?

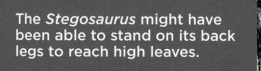

The *Stegosaurus* might have been able to stand on its back legs to reach high leaves.

16

HOW DID A STEGOSAURUS LIVE?

The *Stegosaurus* did not eat meat. It was an **herbivore**. It ate bushes, leaves, and ferns. Some scientists think it could only eat low-growing plants. Other scientists disagree. They think the dinosaur may have reared up on its back legs. Then it could reach higher branches.

Some scientists believe that plate colors helped *Stegosauruses* tell each other apart.

Scientists are not sure what the *Stegosaurus*'s plates were for. Some think the plates helped control the dinosaur's body temperature. Blood vessels in the plates would transfer heat. Plate colors and shapes might have helped identify different *Stegosauruses*.

Ask Questions!

Talk to your friends and family. When they are warm, how do they cool off? When they are cold, what heats them up?

How do scientists learn about *Stegosaurus*? They discover **fossils** and study them. Some fossils have been found in Colorado and Utah in the United States. Fossils showed that plates attached to skin and muscle. They did not attach to bone. There is so much we can learn from dinosaur fossils!

Make a Guess!

How hard is it for scientists to piece fossils together? How do you think they start the process? Ask a teacher, librarian, or other adult for help finding the answers.

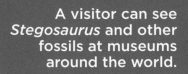

A visitor can see *Stegosaurus* and other fossils at museums around the world.

GLOSSARY

extinct (ek-STINGKT) describing a type of plant or animal that has completely died out

fossils (FAH-suhlz) the preserved remains of living things from thousands or millions of years ago

herbivore (UR-buh-vor) an animal that eats plants rather than other animals

hooves (HOOVZ) the hard coverings over the toes of horses or deer

predators (PRED-uh-turz) animals that live by hunting other animals for food

scutes (SKYOOTS) very large scales on a reptile that often have bone plates underneath that serve as armor

FIND OUT MORE

Books

Braun, Dieter. *Dictionary of Dinosaurs: An Illustrated A to Z of Every Dinosaur Ever Discovered.* New York, NY: Chartwell Books, 2022.

Mara, Wil. *Stegosaurus.* New York, NY: Children's Press, 2012.

Websites

With an adult, learn more online with these suggested searches.

American Museum of Natural History: Stegosaurus
Learn more about *Stegosaurus* and see a photo of a fossil.

Denver Museum of Nature & Science: Prehistoric Journey
Travel through time and watch *Stegosaurus* in action.

INDEX

ABOUT THE AUTHOR

Lucia Raatma has written dozens of books for young readers. She and her family live in the Tampa Bay area of Florida. They enjoy looking at the dinosaur fossils at the local science museum.